EXPRESSIONISM

HEIMO KUCHLING

ARTLINE EDITIONS

FAUVISM — EXPRESSIONISM

Two trends in the visual arts in France and Germany at the beginning of this century have to be mentioned together: Fauvism and expressionism. The "wild beasts" (Fauves) limited themselves to painting. Expressionism, on the other hand, was not just one of many "art styles": it was a movement which included all forms of art. It was the last cultural revolution of the intellectually active middle-classes, it was, as Gottfried Benn put it, a struggle — in a time of political, social, and cultural disruption — "in the middle of this dreadful chaos of the collapse of reality and change of values, forcibly, legitimately and with earnest means for a new picture of humanity" — and a struggle like this unleashed powers, as one can see by looking at the post-expressionist era, which did not exhaust themselves in a regional, temporal, and aesthetically limited "ism". "Collapse of reality" and "change of values" imprint "our era" even more intensely, and so it seems sensible to concern ourselves with expressionism and its effects.

I

In autumn 1888 Vincent van Gogh wrote from Arles to his brother Theo about a painting he was working on, "This time it is quite simply my bedroom, but here the colours must make the subject while their simplification has to give the things a greater style, to suggest peace or sleep generally. The width of the furniture has to express imperturbable tranquility."

In these two sentences the artist mentions a certain form of expression: The things which he presents are formed so that they express the relationship between them and man. Van Gogh talks about an — exaggerated — "width of furniture" and about a "great style": the width of the furniture should express rest. A "great style" only says the absolute necessities about the form of things, it should focus the interest of the viewer on the value of expression given by the artist to the painted objects. Van Gogh did not paint a room at night. Night could rouse fears. In his painting the sun shines into a bright room, a sunny day creates a feeling of ease. The colours are contrasted so that the eye is drawn to the scarlet red of the bed cover: it is surrounded by lime green, dark green, blue, "fresh butter yellow", orange, lilac, and terracotta red. The simple forms of the furniture have only a few, well co-ordinated colour contrasts which enhance each other and have a high emotional value.

Van Gogh developed a style which made his vehement emotional relationship to people and objects strikingly visible and therefore tangible. The "world" is in the true sense of the word seen through the "glasses of temperament" which takes possession of the things with a consuming passion in order to use them as a form of expression. The form of the objects becomes a hieroglyph of a missionary need for communication. "World" becomes the mirror of an "inner world" in which storms of feeling and emotion rage.

"The great style of form also requires a great style of colour," Paula Modersohn-Becker wrote down in her diary on March 8th, 1906. She came from the artists' colony in Worpswede and created — especially in Paris — a picture form in which people, landscapes, and objects have an expression of inner peace. Her "great style" made the painted objects to exemplary objects: the simple, but hard core of the visions becomes visible and the fervour of vital power and vital energy is even expressed where a tender lyricism allows everything to evaporate. "World" and people are in this artist's work in a relation to each other where the "world" is present because the artist fervently strives for an artistic conquest of the subject in which her formal and worldly experiences are expressed.

Vincent van Gogh and Paula Modersohn-Becker formed two varieties of an art form which was called "expressionistic art". The one presented itself as a stormy emotional world seizure in which the one who experiences plays a bigger role than the experience itself. The other as a world statement in which the person making the statement steps behind that what has been said about the world — worldly experiences and not world seizure is the driving force behind art.

Apart from the "great style" and a reduction in contrasts, van Gogh employed a further medium for his increased personal statement which is very characteristic for his painting — a

Blaue Reiter developed an analytic art in contact with the cubists and the futurists. August Macke managed the most uninterrupted transition from Fauvism to analytic art. Averse to every narrow and strict doctrine, he was only a hesitant analyst when he found it necessary for the explanation of his formal language. His purest and most unbroken paintings are his later, non-analytic works in which a very clear compromised, strongly assertive figuration together with a brilliant, harmonious colourfulness creates a tight picture form. These pictures are counted among the most valued treasures in German art along with the later works from Modersohn-Becker and the "window paintings" from Oskar Schlemmer, also later works. Analytic art only took over the colourfulness of the Fauvists. However, it is remarkable that even in the analytical paintings by Marc such as "Tower of the Blue Horses" or "Animal Destinies" expressiveness prevails.

III

Fauvism cannot always be distinctly separated from expressionism: Many pictures by Kees van Dongen could be counted as belonging to Fauvism as well as to expressionism; Kirchner and Heckel and even Schmidt-Rottluff used less colour in their expressionistic phase. The actual catalyst for the transition from Fauvism to expressionism in Germany is probably the work done by Edvard Munch who had several exhibitions in Germany between 1899 and 1912 which were enthusiastically accepted by the youth.

Already in 1893 Edvard Munch painted the picture "The Scream" which was very significant for expressionism. In a red-green and blue-yellow contrast in which green is used sparingly and where fire-red dominates there are a flaming sky, deep-blue water, mountains, spits of land, and a bridge on which a figure stands in the foreground like a licking flame, the mouth wide-open, the hands pressed to the head — the whole painting is a single scream. The picture figuration consists of wavy, curving, and straight lined areas which associate objects with colourfulness and context, but which, when isolated become abstract. Depth is obtained through the perspectively drawn bridge and the difference in height of the figures.

Red, orange, and yellow are screaming, aggressive colours, the curvatures swing in the excited rhythm and the bridge railings cut sharply into the picture area. Blue and green make the tumult bearable, and at the same time exaggerate it by the contrast. The face of the figure is not physiognomically distinguished, it is in its outline and inside form nothing but fear and screaming.

Fear, screaming, and inner burning are the subjective expressions for a world in which a "revaluation of values" is in course. The vehement arrival of the industrial age, radical changes in society, and the first phase in the mechanization of life rocked traditional forms of living and thinking, made habits which had been handed down break apart, without the new, promising shore being in sight. Munch's personal fear of illness and death became in his art an existential transpersonal fear, such as exists in times of external and internal upheaval. Society felt as if it was standing on insecure ground, and the individual saw the world bursting at the seams and panicked, and panic was responsible for the scream: in Munch who represented his contemporaries. This scream first came from the North, because man is more exposed to night than daylight there and therefore is always close to fear. Personal anxiety shown in works of art increased to world anxiety — to the expression of a world anxiety. This fear shook the world, made it burn.

If the French Fauvism was an outside impulse for German expressionism the Munch's work came from "inside". The French appealed to the senses, to the eyes they delivered pictorial means, especially a chromatic value of colourfulness. Munch addressed the soul directly, the "inner world" of man. He offered a unique example, extending beyond his person, that it is possible to share fears, mental duress, inner strife, threats, and emotions pictorially. As Benn talks of a "grasping of words from tension" it can be said of Munch that he used a grasping of figures and colours from tension. Tension which arises in the artist in his clash with the world in which he has been placed is an absolute necessity for an essential, expressive work.

Van Gogh's expressionism originated from the missionary urge to lead a tyrannized and burdened people from the darkness into light. Munch, on the other hand, painted from an inner need and inflamed the whole world with his inner fire and so became the direct spark for German expressionism.

The fin-de-siècle mood which preceded expressionism and the speed of industrialisation made many artists tired of civilization. Herder and the Romantics collected folk-stories, folk-songs, myths, and fairy-tales from many different nations which became a new source of poetry. The artists of the Pont-Aven school, especially Gauguin, studied verre églomisé and folk-art as did the artists of Der Blaue Reiter later. The ethnologists reported of "primitive races" whose products were offered as curiosities. Gauguin eventually went to the West Indies and then to the South Sea isles to liberate himself from the "frightening form of expression of degenerate races" and to find the sources of life and art. He paid for his idea with his life. Van Gogh had to make do with the Provence which fascinated him, and the expressionists were satisfied with "primitive" sculptures which they used as requisites for still lifes directly or as models for their own sculptures.

Although the fascination which emanated from the "primitive" cultures was so great, the harvest which it brought the civilized artist was very small. Picasso interpreted the "negro art" most astutely. He concentrated on the repertoire of form in the art and recognised in this the creative power of geometric figures. It is not possible to have direct access to the "inner" content of this art, its sources are not obvious and therefore cannot be evaluated.

The attempt to gain new impulse from religion, or more exactly from religious themes, which Nolde, Schmidt-Rottluff, and Rohls, later Morgner and in France Georges Rouault undertook, did not go beyond the thematic either.

These sojourns into foreign and borderlands, this fleeing from civilization and from the tensions in intellectual and political happenings of the time show unmistakably that expressionism comes from these tensions, that they were sources, that it could not flee from the "cross of its time" under which it was born. The cross which Christ bore was not

11

that of the expressionists and the myths of the "primitive races" came from a world which is unattainable for us. But the fact that expressionism cannot be detached from its "time" from the tensions in the society in which it was formed, is an example of its authenticity, of its historical necessity.

Expressionism — its main period was from around 1910 to 1920 — has many different variations. For example, a peasant-earthbound quality with Nolde, Barlach and Schmidt-Rottluff, a metropolitan quality with Kirchner and Heckel, a psychological one with Oskar Kokoschka, and a lyrical one with Otto Mueller and Christian Rohlfs.

It seems contradictory to talk of a peasant-earthbound style of expressionism. But it should be considered that especially the person who comes from a farming community such as Emil Nolde is harder hit by the clash with inconsistent civilization.

"Nolde, the old soul," Paul Klee called him and said of him, "when he paints it is with a human hand, a hand not without heaviness, in a way not without blemish. The mysterious fullblooded hand of the lower region." From this region Nolde created his glowing, brilliant colourfulness, it also forced him, however, to an excessive supply of illuminating power and contrast effect so that he often crossed the borders of artistic credibility: it is the "way not without blemish" — his aquarelles and etchings are free of these "blemishes". But in his woodcuts the danger of overdoing the intensity of expression is always acute.

The expressionists took over the art of woodcuts from Munch who cut simple figures into rough grained wood. The harsh black and white contrast, the rough cutting technique and the inclusion of the wood-grain in the form were an increase of expression in graphic art which the woodprint did not allow.

Terror and aggression appear in Karl Schmidt-Rottluff's work in a hard and awkward style of drawing, in violent contrasts of colour, in an angular manner of woodcutting in an almost unbearable tension. The faces he creates, as those from Nolde, freeze to become masks; even the sun appears to give

Unrest and fear and aggression which had become genre motifs were opposed by the exceptionally psychological expressionism of the Austrian Oskar Kokoschka. The springboard to Kokoschka's expression was the late work by Egon Schiele. Schiéle who was first under the influence of the fin-de-siècle mood of Gustav Klimt, soon experienced the corruption and morbidity of Viennese society in those days — this was the base from which Sigmund Freud developed his psycho-analysis and theory of neuroses. In a still life Kokoschka brought together symbols which elucidate his early representations of people: a skinned sheep — the exposed inner nature; the amphibian — feeling around in the darkness of the unknown; the white mouse — the flight from light; and the tortoise, which retires into itself when in danger. A hyacinth, the flower which gives off a numbing aroma overreaches, a symbol itself, the other symbols. Kokoschka "smelled" his models — as he said himself — scented their hidden instinctive and spiritual qualities and exposed them.

IV

Gottfried Benn's statement about the generation of expressionism being prepared for a short life is only relevant to the expressionism which appeared like a jet of flame; the poet himself later spoke of "Phase II" of expressionism. The contents of reality, even the gain in reality compared to Fauvism and Art Nouveau, the conquest over an aestheticism under the pressure of an explosive social situation gave expressionism creative power. The deed of van Gogh, Munch, and the true expressionists to have changed "world inner space" (Rilke) into a picture world and given form to fears, aggression, pressures, and escape from pressures became a founding act. Expressionism is not an abstract idealism which could lose the ground from which it developed; expressionism cannot elevate itself so above the factors which bind it to reality. When reality attacks the artist, where it conquers him, endangers or — on the contrary — where he obtains substantial powers from it which enrich him, it becomes an expression, it forces him to express his experiences and sensations. Art which does not limit itself to splendid representation, to devotional painting, or to the settling of inner-artistic — formal — problems is expressive art, the seeds which expressionism sowed came up in it. Changes in form correspond to changes in reality.

At first it looked as if expressionism would fade away after 1920. The head of the Brücke artists, Kirchner, had to move away from the city to the Swiss mountains because of tuberculosis. There his colourfulness became more vivid and deep, but the vulcanic ground of the metropolis had been taken away from him, the area of tension from which his art drew its power. The methods which he had developed were not suitable for the artistic interpretation of the mountains and their people. Overcome by a psychosis caused by his tuberculosis, he finally entered into an imagined competitive struggle with Picasso which caused his own artistic end — a tragic fate.

The second generation of expressionism could not compensate the collapse of the "Brücke" either: No matter how they tried, they could not emulate the authenticity of their ideals and they were so close to those ideals that they could not completely remove themselves from them, something which would have been necessary for finding a new path or their own form of language. Heckel soon tended towards a naturalising form composition and Schmidt-Rottluff ended up with a mixture between naturalism — representation of light and shadow — and expressive drawing in his late work. Pankok and Felixmüller soon saw themselves with no backing, Morgner died in World War I, Nolde and Barlach who were able to remain true to themselves, drew from sources which were only available to them — they were not able to form a "school". Kirchner had a school in Switzerland, but it remained a regional event.

German expressionism radiated onto the art in other countries. The Austrian Kokoschka has already been mentioned; however, he remained an isolated case. The realism of the Austrian art in the 19th century was effective into the 20th century and characterized the expressive art in Austria: Herbert Boeckl painted Cézanne orientated paintings with a heavy hand, they have an expressive-realistic character until his abstract late works. Rudolf Wacker, one of the founders of "magic realism" also had a powerful expressive phase. The late paintings by Josef Dobrowsky are softer, less clear, but exceptionally picturesque. From the younger artists one could mention Rudolf Korunka who creates a burlesque, vivacious-stiff puppet world. Hans Plank's work belongs to the pastoral area which he portrayed in a realistic expressionism in woodcuts and in paintings. The sculptor, graphic artist, and painter Alfred Hrdlicka, who is socio-critically orientated, works with expressive distortions of the figures. Norbert Grebmer paints expressive interpretations of people and landscapes. The sculptor Walter Salzmann portrays in an expressive formal language the existential threats to man in today's society. Otto Jungwirth sketches and paints the humdrum life of the city dweller in a deliberately clumsy way which makes it very expressive.

Expressionism is remarkable above all in France. Georges Rouault has already been mentioned: his window-type full-blooded painting, which shows whores, clowns, and Christ, is expressive-introvert. Chaim Soutine painted with a furor reminiscent of van Gogh, Marcel Grommaire's paintings are cold, affected and have a strangely stiff dynamic. One can recognize clear expressive tendencies of an attacking kind even in the neo-realist Bernard Lorjou.

A look at the immediate sphere of influence of expressionism in the narrow sense shows something important: Expressionism is not tied to one type of form. It is not limited to the real expressionism; this is just the first type of expression formed under certain historical conditions. "Phase II" of expressionism, shifted to the visual arts, is more poylmorphic than "Phase I". The expression is not limited anymore to the historical expressionism, it is apparent in other "isms" as, for example, in the new "realistic" directions, and something which will still be mentioned, in formally orientated flows.

Now back to Germany. When, for example, Käthe Kollwitz cut in wood she used a technique and a form language which would have been unthinkable without the expressionists, the same as her sculptures remind us of Barlach's, although she is "more realistic" than the expressionists. Although the new objectivity can be seen as a reaction to expressionism, which suited the political parties by being unpolitical, it received expressive tendencies — expecially from Otto Dix. The fact that "New Objectivity", "neo-realism", "Verism", and "magic realism" are interchangeable titles for — apparently — one and the same art direction shows that it deals with a special realism, and what is special is that expressive and surreal elements are contained in it. An aggressive form language serves a presentation which attacks politically. Expressionism offers this more than any other language. In this the poster-type, the shortened version of committed art, is also asserted. Both can be found in the revolutionary Mexican art: realistic-expressive as with José Clemente Orozco or naturalistic-expressive as with David Alfaro Siqueiros or cubist-expressive as with Rufino Tamayo who translated Munch's "scream" into Mexican-cubist art.

When Max Beckmann discovered the horror of war while serving as a soldier in the Medical Corps in World War I, he recognized that the impressionistic means which he was capable of were not enough to express the reality of this horror. He felt forced to develop another form language, and here he was helped by those movements which he had previously sharply attacked, namely Fauvism, expressionism, Der Blaue Reiter. Expressing reality does not mean recording the impression which it gives — it means much more: It is concerned with intensity, with a strong expressive enhancement of what is seen, a composition has to be gained which relates directly to the viewer, which jumps at him. Reality only becomes obvious in such compositions. Beckmann did the right thing: he did not borrow any available formal language, instead he purified the impressionist drawing to a precise lineation, transposed the figures to sharply accentuated figuration, initially took the colour back to its grey value and then successively increased the colours, sometimes creating hard contrasts. Figuration and colourfulness combined to a compact, close, and completely emphatic form language in contrast to that of, for example, Kirchner's, but it is nonetheless of a sharply attacking expressiveness, which still marks his literary conceived late works.

War also shook another artist who worked on a completely different level from Beckmann: Pablo Picasso. Analytic and synthetic cubism, but also the classicism of this artist concerned exclusively formal questions of pictorial representation — a contrast to expressionism which asked the questions about form only in connection with questions about increased expression: "Guernica" undoubtedly is a synthetic-cubist painting, but its modus of representation reaches far beyond the borders of one specific problem of form: the cubist form assets and the cubist methods of representation were first used in this painting for an aggressive-expressive pictorial statement — and they suited it magnificently. Simultaneous spatial views of the represented objects, separation of line and colour area — here clair obscure areas — areas out of perspective especially forced the drastic representation of shock, horror, explosion, and destruction with their unnaturalness. The artist who created still lifes, informal scenes, landscapes, and scenes created for purely aesthetic reasons, through staggering events in the Spanish Civil War and World War II, suddenly became an artist who concerned himself with the political and militant happenings, with death and destruction in his time. From this concern, he created expressive paintings, works in which reality is comprehendingly and suggestively represented. Such as the cat which tears the bird to pieces, or in the bull which pokes around in the intestines of a horse, or directly as in the "Crying Woman".

Under the same circumstances, the sculptor Jacques Lipchitz created sculptures during World War II which are definitely expressive, such as the man killing a cockerel; symbolism does not exclude expressionism.

Also the work of the Belgian Constant Permekes proves that cubist forms, even if not fully developed, and expressionism do not exclude each other. With Flemish heaviness, stereoscopic areas push each other to an expressive composition: farmers at a table, or a mother pig with her piglets appear to raise themselves laboriously out of the damp earth.

V

What has been said here about expressionism is meant to suggest that expressionistic forms are not, as is much too often assumed, an outflow of youthful Sturm und Drang. It does not arise from subjective acts of violence either, it is rather more the fruit of extraordinary external and internal tensions, it struggles for "a new picture of humanity" in a world which threatens to destroy itself. But all the dangers which lie in expressionism itself have a part in this process of destruction: giving oneself over to intoxication and ecstasy, the enthronement of hallucination, the inclination to behave pre-logically, the division between thinking and feeling, "spirit" and "soul". The spiritual condition of the "primitive" peoples cannot be reproduced by a highly civilized people. Every attempt in this direction leads to a disorganization of the created, to a dissolution of the laboriously obtained moral and ethical values. It has to founder on a false romanticism, on its absurdity.

A new picture of humanity cannot be achieved by one or two generations — it is a process which generation after generation has to work on. It is a picture which has to be wrung from the distorted picture of man.

Expressionism, expressiveness is not a youthful folly or illness which has to be quickly surmounted — only a misunderstood expressionism has to be overcome. Subjective arbitrary acts, excessive painting or distorting figures as one pleases are not expressionism or expression, they just come from pretended tensions and are mostly self-deceit.

"Phase II" of expressionism is not a "pacified" expressionism nor has it become more bourgeois so to speak, but rather it continually increases in its contents of reality. That means gain of the world through a progression of knowledge of the "inner self", of the spiritual powers and power-field constellations, which dominate the world in which we live. Subjectivity is driven so far forward that it transcends itself, that it becomes a common expression. Munch delivered a first sign after his "nervous breakdown". The representation of the human form becomes "more objective", the dynamic of the internal events more far-reaching, the composition becomes wide and gains in depth. Fear, shock, tension are all still there, but they do not allow the world to stiffen to a mask, they move it, they are powers which create streams of life. Paula Modersohn-Becker's work presents an even earlier anticipation of "Phase II": Her "great style": The result of a very intensive and consistant struggle for the transposition of reality into picture form, in which existence becomes being, in which the being of things, humans, the world is expressed. It is not expression for expression's sake for extremely critical aesthetic formulations — Benn himself indulged in those — it deals much more with the gain of a supporting base for art and with an aesthetically encroaching ethical attitude. A work can only arise from such an attitude in which reality has been legitimately related to the human spirit. The way there is now further than ever before.

One station on this way is the hitherto existing work of the painter and woodcutter Werner Berg. He recognized the dangers which lie in expressionism — intoxication, ecstasy, menacing feeling — the uncontrollable, and established himself as a farmer in Kärnten. His early work announces the excitement about his new pastoral living area which is so rich in picture motifs in an almost Fauvist expressive style. His later work increasingly shows the fortifying form of the "inner face" of the farming people and their landscape. The pictorial language becomes clearer, more transparent and because of this more deeply gripping in its expression. Picture plan, figuration and colourfulness tend towards a unison between the objects and the expression of nature of the artist's world as he discovers with increasing intensity.

Gottfried Benn understood by expressionism, "new picture of humanity", and "Phase II" something different from the author. These terms have been used because they make sense as such and because they come from an expressionistic poet. The painters went a different way from that which was described by Benn.

ILLUSTRATIONS

28

29

Table I

KARL SCHMIDT-ROTTLUFF
Still Life with Sea Holly
Painting, 1913
Private collection

33

34

Table II

ERICH HECKEL
Farmstead
Painting, 1909
Hessisches Landesmuseum, Darmstadt

43

52

Table III

MAX PECHSTEIN
Thaw
Painting, 1922
Museum am Ostwall, Dortmund

58

63

Table IV

ERNST LUDWIG KIRCHNER
Church in Monstein
Painting, 1916/17
Hessisches Landesmuseum, Darmstadt

71

Table V

OTTO MUELLER
Gypsy with Child in front of a Waggon Wheel
("Gipsy Madonna")
Colour lithograph, 1927, from the "Gypsy Portfolio"

100

Emil Nolde

104

Table VI

EMIL NOLDE
His Ancestors
Painting, 1919
Hessisches Landesmuseum, Darmstadt

105

TABLE VII

HEINRICH CAMPENDONK
Animals
Painting, 1917
Leopold Hösch Museum, Düren

119

131

132

14.8.31

140

146

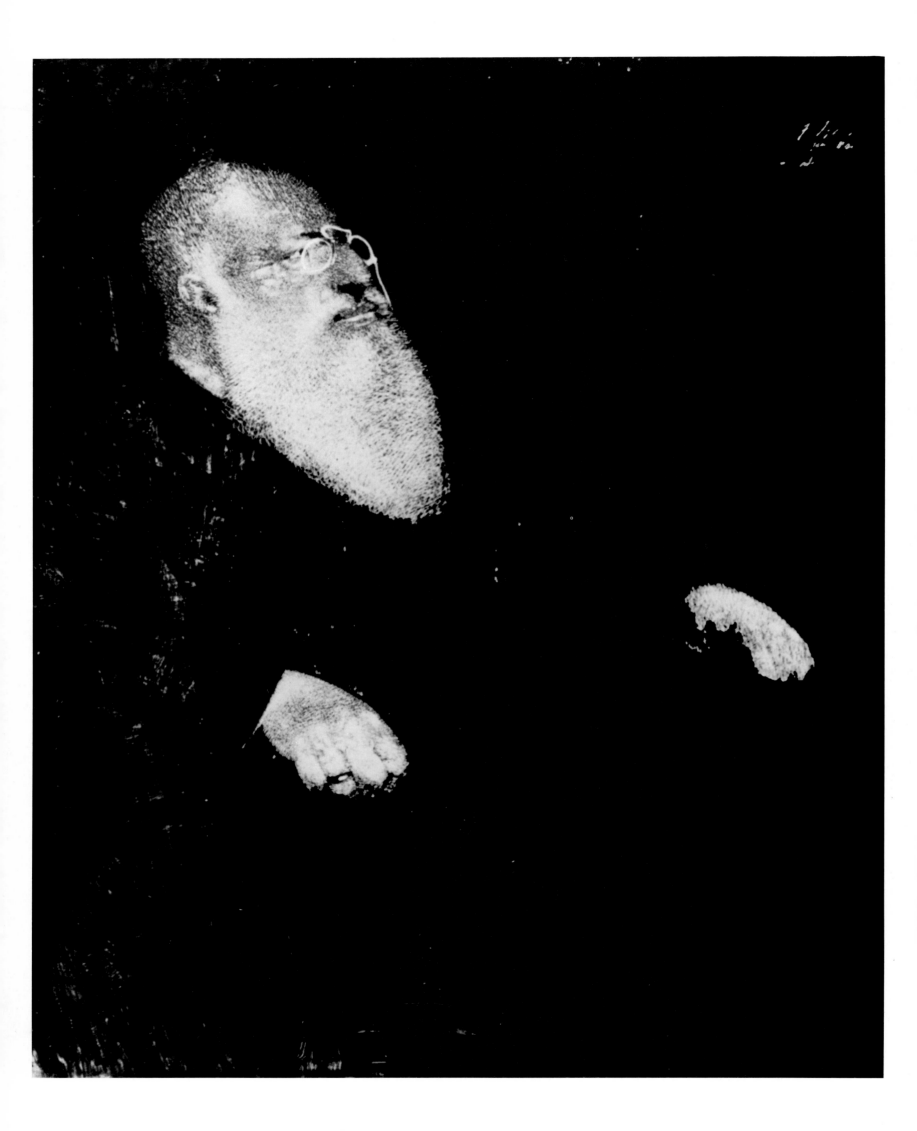

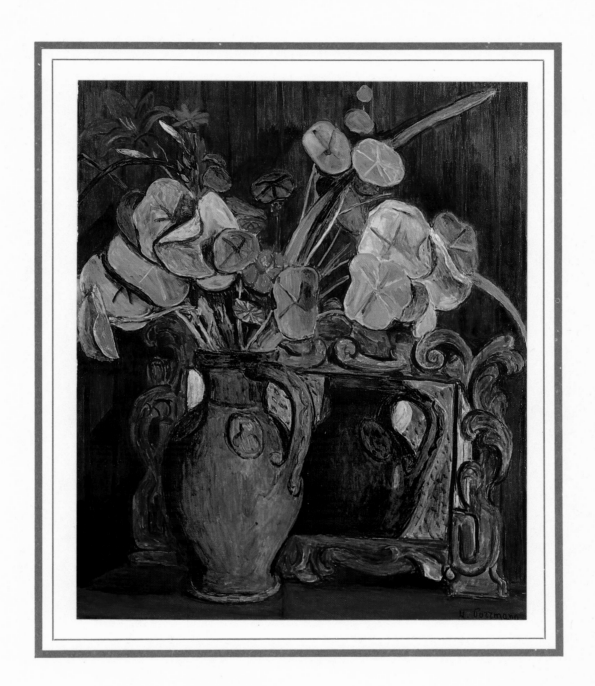

TABLE VIII

HANS PURRMANN
Still Life with Nasturtium
Painting, 1952
Staatsgalerie, Stuttgart

149

150

Handdrack

152

LIST OF ARTISTS
IN ALPHABETICAL ORDER

BARLACH, Ernst
1870 Wedel (Holstein) — 1938 Rostock

Barlach was equally important as a poet, graphic artist, and sculptor. He became known, however, through his powerful sculptures, the expressive forms which have religious intimacy as well as an elementary closeness to the people.
Fig. p. 143

BECKMANN, Max
1884 Leipzig — 1950 New York

Beckmann was above all a realist whose paintings are visions, screams, comparisons, impressed by the events of two wars. Characterizing him as an expressionist would be too limiting; expression was for him in its full crassness just a means of expression for his warnings of the destructive forces.
Fig. pp. 135, 136, 137, 138, 139

BERG, Werner
1904 Elberfeld — 1981 Rutarhof/Kärnten

Berg's work is distinguished by an unusually high and convincing content of reality. He wanted to tie art to life and withdrew to a farm which he ran and which was at the same time a source and thematic area of his extensive works.
Fig. p. 59

CAMPENDONK, Heinrich
1889 Krefeld — 1957 Amsterdam

Campendonk worked in Germany till his expulsion in 1933, the last years as professor at the Dusseldorf Academy. He became one of the most influential artists of German expressionism through his work in the circle of "DerBlaue Reiter". His powerful graphic works are especially famous.
Fig. pp. 112, 113, Table VII

DIX, Otto
1891 Untermhaus near Gera — 1969 Hemmenhofen (Lake Constance)

With his later works Dix was regarded as the main representative of German post-expressionism. Like M. Beckmann and G. Grosz he is mainly a realist. With his exceptional ability and the technique of the Old Masters he negated any charm to arouse and denounce with every pencil stroke.
Fig. p. 132

DONGEN, Kees van
1877 Delfshaven near Rotterdam — 1968 Monaco

Dongen is one of the most important representatives of modern Dutch art. At first he was influenced by the impressionists, but he joined the Fauves in Paris in 1906 and later was a member of the "Brücke" in Dresden. His paintings are characterized by exceptionally intensive colours.
Fig. p. 151

PURRMANN, Hans
1880 Speyer — 1966 Basel

Purrmann, who was originally an admirer of the impressionists, was deeply impressed by H. Matisse who he got to know while travelling. Together they founded an art school. Although he was a contemporary of the expressionists. Purrmann was always connected with the French school of the Fauves.
Fig. Table VIII

ROHLFS, Christian
1849 Niendorf — 1938 Hagen

As fitting for his age, Rohlfs works emanated from impressionism. Impressed by Cézanne and van Gogh, he joined the expressionists, painted for a short time with Nolde and soon found his own style in strongly expressive graphic art, subtle flower paintings, and religious themes.
Fig. pp. 94/95, 96, 97, 98

RUDOLPH, Wilhelm
1889 Chemnitz — lives in Dresden

Rudolph portends the influence of the impressionists in his work. He is mainly a painter of portraits, landscapes, and animals. In his graphic art, however, he works expressionistically with woodcuts as a special means of expression.
Fig. p. 152

SCHLEMMER, Oskar
1888 Stuttgart — 1943 Baden Baden

Schlemmer's artistic works are varied. He was a painter and sculptor and received the control of the sculpture and stage workshops in the "Bauhaus" in Weimar. The sculptural form always dominated his paintings.
Fig. p. 140

SCHMIDT-ROTTLUFF, Karl
1884 Rottluff near Chemnitz — 1976 Berlin

As a founder member of the artistic community "Brücke", he is regarded as one of the most important artists of German expressionism. His work is characterized in colour and form by an expressive liberality. The expression of contrast can especially be seen in his graphic work.
Fig. pp. 27, 28, 29, 30/31, 32, 33, 34/35, Table I

SLUJTERS, Jan
1881 Herzogenbosch — 1957 Amsterdam

Slujters is counted among the leading Dutch expressionists. He was at first influenced by the French neo-impressionists, but later — drawing on van Gogh's heritage — he used the interpretation possibilities of expressionism.
Fig. p. 141

STARK, Karl
1921 Glojach — lives in Vienna

Stark studied sculpture and first discovered painting in this way. The powerful paint application and the strong expressiveness of his paintings are described as "expressionistic", he himself, however, subsumed expressionism along with other influences in order that his own work could become clearly outlined.

Fig. p. 150

WOUTERS, Rik
1882 Malines — 1916 Amsterdam

Wouters was a painter and sculptor. He educated himself from French impressionism and later got to know the Fauves who influenced him strongly. His work was eventually decisive for Flemish Fauvism.

Fig. p. 144

TABLE OF ILLUSTRATIONS

On the Title Page
Erich Heckel
Reclining Nude, Fränzi
Colour woodcut, 1910

25
Paula Modersohn-Becker
Self-Portrait with Twig of Camellia
Painting, around 1907
Museum Folkwang, Essen

26
Cesar Klein
Fishing Boats on the Beach
Woodcut

27
Karl Schmidt-Rottluff
Fishing Boats
Woodcut, 1913

28
Karl Schmidt-Rottluff
Landscape with Two Women
Painting, 1919
Kunstmuseum, Dusseldorf

29
Karl Schmidt-Rottluff
Towers of Stralsund
Woodcut, 1912

30/31
Karl Schmidt-Rottluff
Reclining Model
Colour woodcut, 1911

32
Karl Schmidt-Rottluff
Woman with Her Hair Undone
Woodcut, 1913

33
Karl Schmidt-Rottluff
Heads I
Woodcut, 1911

34/35
Karl Schmidt-Rottluff
Ponte Nomentano
Aquarelle, 1930
Von der Heydt-Museum,
Wuppertal

36
Alfred Kubin
Man and Woman Talking
Pencil drawing
Staatliche Graphische Sammlung,
Munich

37
Erich Heckel
Girl in front of a Mirror
Dry-point engraving, 1920

38
Erich Heckel
White Horses
Colour woodcut, 1912

39
Erich Heckel
Portrait of a Man
(Self-Portrait)
Colour woodcut, 1919

40
Erich Heckel
Woman Sitting
Woodcut, 1913

41
Erich Heckel
Woman Kneeling at a Stone
Woodcut, 1913

42/43
Erich Heckel
Saxon Village
Painting, 1910
Von der Heydt-Museum,
Wuppertal

44
Erich Heckel
On the Beach
Woodcut, 1923

45
Erich Heckel
Bathing Women in the Rushes
(Detail)
Painting, 1909
Kunstmuseum, Dusseldorf

46
Otto Pankok
Self-Portrait
Woodcut, 1958

47
Otto Pankok
Maxim Gorki
Woodcut, 1947

48
Max Pechstein
Portrait of the Artist's Wife
Painting, 1910
Museum Ludwig, Cologne

49
Max Pechstein
Lady with a Fur
Etching, undated

50/51
Max Pechstein
Three Fishermen
Colour Woodcut, 1923

52
Max Pechstein
Portrait of Male Head with Hat
Woodcut, 1911

53
Max Pechstein
Three Fishing Boats
Woodcut, 1912

54/55
Max Pechstein
Rising Sun
Painting, 1933
Saarland Museum, Saarbrücken

56
Max Pechstein
Head of a Child
Lithograph, 1916

57
Lyonel Feininger
Lady with Green Eyes
Painting, 1915
Private collection

58
Hans Plank
Mother Leaving
Woodcut, 1969

59
Werner Berg
Woman Walking away
Woodcut, 1948

60
Ernst Ludwig Kirchner
Street Scene
Colour Woodcut,
1922

61
Ernst Ludwig Kirchner
Five Cocottes
Woodcut, 1913

62/63
Ernst Ludwig Kirchner
Bathing Women Throwing Reeds
Colour woodcut, 1910

64
Ernst Ludwig Kirchner
Old Peasant
Woodcut, 1918

65
Ernst Ludwig Kirchner
Old Man from the Alps with
Black Hat and Beard
Woodcut, 1919

66/67
Ernst Ludwig Kirchner
Reclining Woman
Painting, around 1910
Kunstmuseum, Dusseldorf

68
Ernst Ludwig Kirchner
Head of Miss Hardt
Woodcut, 1914

69
Ernst Ludwig Kirchner
Young Girl
Woodcut, 1919

70/71
Ernst Ludwig Kirchner
Spruce Trees in the Mountains
(Wildboden)
Aquarelle on top of pencil drawing,
approx. 1924
Staedelsches Kunstinstitut,
Frankfort

72
Conrad Felixmüller
The Mining Engineer
Woodcut, 1922

73
Conrad Felixmüller
Lovers in front of a Factory Site
Quill drawing, 1922
Owned by the administration of
the estate

74
Otto Mueller
Portrait of a Gypsy in Profile to
the Right
Colour lithograph from the "Gypsy
Portfolio", 1927

75
Otto Mueller
Portrait of Gypsy Woman and
Adolescent Girl
Colour lithograph from the "Gypsy
Portfolio", 1927

76
Otto Mueller
Two Bathing Girls, the Left one
with Hat
Lithograph, 1921/22

77
Otto Mueller
Nude in front of the Mirror
Lithograph, 1924

78/79
Otto Mueller
Bathing Girls in the Grass
Painting, around 1920
Von der Heydt-Museum,
Wuppertal

80
Otto Mueller
Self-Portrait
Lithograph, 1921

81
Otto Mueller
Nude Standing under Trees
Painting, 1915
Kunstmuseum, Dusseldorf

82
Oskar Kokoschka
Girl's Head
(Ruth Landshoff)
Lithograph, 1922

83
Oskar Kokoschka
Portrait of a Gentleman (Ivar von
Lücken)
Lithograph, 1918

84
Oskar Kokoschka
The Persian
Painting, 1923
Leopold Hoesch Museum, Düren

85
Oskar Kokoschka
Pegasus
Lithograph, 1966

86/87
Edvard Munch
Lovers in the Forest
Colour woodcut, 1915

88
Edvard Munch
Girl Holding Her Hands in Front
of Her Mouth
Charcoal drawing, after 1912
Munch-Museet, Oslo

89
Edvard Munch
The Scream
Painting, 1893
Nasjonallgalleriet, Oslo

90
Edvard Munch
Horse
Charcoal drawing, around 1912
Munch-Museet, Oslo

91
Edvard Munch
Galloping Horse
Etching, 1915

92
Edvard Munch
Lumberjack
Painting, 1913
Munch-Museet, Oslo

93
Ferdinand Hodler
Lumberjack
Chalk lithograph, 1910

94/95
Christian Rohlfs
The Gate in Dinkelsbühl
Painting, 1924
Von der Heydt-Museum, Wuppertal

96
Christian Rohlfs
Three Women (Unnamed)
Linocut, 1912

97
Christian Rohlfs
Autumn Tree
Painting, 1917
Von der Heydt-Museum, Wuppertal

98
Christian Rohlfs
Large Head (Unnamed)
Woodcut, 1922

99
Emil Nolde
Prophet
Woodcut, 1912

100
Emile Nolde
Anemones and Amaryllis
Aquarelle, undated
Staatliche Graphische Sammlung,
Munich

101
Emil Nolde
Sailing Boat with Smoke
Etching, 1910

102/103
Emil Nolde
Mill on the Water
Colour lithograph, 1926
(Unicum in this colour combination)
Staedelsches Kunstinstitut,
Frankfurt

104
Emil Nolde
Kneeling Girl
Etching, 1905

105
Emile Nolde
In the Morning
Etching, 1907

106
Alexej von Jawlensky
The White Feather
Painting, 1909
Staatsgalerie, Stuttgart

107
Alexej von Jawlensky
Girl with Peonies
Painting, 1909
Von der Heydt-Museum, Wuppertal

108
Alexej von Jawlensky
Woman's Head
Lithograph, 1912

109
Wassily Kandinsky
Cover of the Almanac "Der Blaue
Reiter"
Woodcut, 1912

110/111
Wassily Kandinsky
Bavarian Landscape with Church
Painting, 1908
Von der Heydt-Museum, Wuppertal

112
Heinrich Campendonk
Sitting Girl with Stag
Woodcut, 1916

113
Heinrich Campendonk
Standing Nude with Flowers and
Frogs
Woodcut, around 1914

114/115
Franz Marc
Resting Horses
Colour lithograph (enlarged),
1912

116
Franz Marc
Tiger
Woodcut, 1912

117
Franz Marc
Tiger
Painting, 1912
Städtische Galerie im Lehnbach-
haus, Munich

118
Franz Marc
Two Cats
Colour lithograph for an exhibition
placard, 1909/10

119
Franz Marc
Two Horses
Colour lithograph, 1908

120
Franz Marc
Tower of the Blue Horses
Painting, 1913
(Missing or destroyed)
Reproduction according to a
coloured Hanfstaengl-print

121
Franz Marc
Drinking Horse
Woodcut (Enlarged), 1912

122
Franz Marc
Deer in the Forest I
Painting, 1912
Städtische Galerie im Lehnbach-
haus, Munich

123
Franz Marc
Deers in the Forest II
Painting, 1913
Staatliche Kunsthalle, Karlsruhe

124
August Macke
Greeting
Linocut, 1912

125
August Macke
Bathing Women
Painting, 1913
Bayerische Staatsgemälde-
sammlungen, Munich

126
August Macke
Sailing Yacht
Sketchbook No. 50, drawing No. 52
Rheindorf, 1913
Landesmuseum für Kunst und
Kulturgeschichte, Münster

127
August Macke
Boat on the Rhine near Rheindorf
Sketchbook No. 50, drawing No. 36
Rheindorf, 1913
Landesmuseum für Kunst und
Kulturgeschichte, Münster

128
August Macke
Four Girls
Painting, around 1912
Kunstmuseum, Dusseldorf

129
August Macke
Three Girls in the Forest
Pencil drawing, 1913
Städtisches Kunstmuseum, Bonn

130/131
August Macke
With a Yellow Jacket
Aquarelle, 1913
Museum der Stadt, Ulm

132
Otto Dix
Girl with Sunflower
Lithograph, 1958

133
Carl Hofer
The Lute-Player
Painting, 1931
Leopold Hoesch Museum, Düren

134
Georg Grosz
Contrasts
Ink drawing, around 1917
Graphische Sammlung der Staats-
galerie, Stuttgart

135
Max Beckmann
Self-Portrait with Cat and Lamp
Lithograph, 1920

136
Max Beckmann
Quappie
Painting, 1944
Kunstmuseum, Dusseldorf

137
Max Beckmann
The Big Bridge
Etching, 1922

138
Max Beckmann
Woman with Candle
Woodcut, 1920

139
Max Beckmann
Minette
Etching, 1922

140
Oskar Schlemmer
Three Figures
Pencil and quill drawing, 1931
Kunstmuseum, Basel,
Kupferstichkabinett

141
Jan Sluijters
Mrs van der Vuurst
Painting, 1914
Stedelijk Museum, Amsterdam

142
Käthe Kollwitz
Working-Class Woman with Boy in
her Arms
Lithograph, 1931

143
Ernst Barlach
Mourning Woman
Drawing, 1930
E. Barlach Nachlaß, Ratzeburg

144
Rik Wouters
Woman at the Window
Painting, 1915
Koninklijk Museum, Antwerpen

145
Gabriele Münter
Female Half-Figure Standing
Pencil drawing, around 1925
Städtische Galerie im Lenbach-
haus, Munich

146
Paul Klee
Without Title (Region in the
Eifenau near Bern)
Painting, 1906
Nachlaß-Sammlung Felix Klee, Bern

147
Paul Klee
Girl with Jugs
Painting, 1910
Nachlaß-Sammlung Felix Klee, Bern

148
Paul Klee
Portrait of My Father
Verre églomisé, 1906
Nachlaß-Sammlung Felix Klee, Bern

149
Paul Klee
The Drunkard
Etching, 1907

150
Karl Stark
Yellow flowers in a White Vase
Gouache, 1973
Private collection

151
Kees van Dongen
Nude Girl
Painting, around 1910
Von der Heydt-Museum, Wuppertal

152
Wilhelm Rudolph
Old Man
Woodcut